Traveling
In Grandma's Day

by Valerie Weber
and Patti Baker

❧ Carolrhoda Books, Inc./Minneapolis

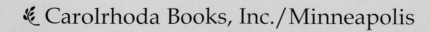

Carolrhoda Books, Inc., A Division of the Lerner Publishing Group
241 First Avenue North, Minneapolis, MN 55401 U.S.A.

Website address: www.lernerbooks.com

Planning and production by Discovery Books
Edited by Faye Gardner
Text designed by Ian Winton
Illustrations by Stuart Lafford
Commissioned photography by Sabine Beaupré and Jim Wend

The publishers would like to thank Patti Baker for her help in the preparation of this book.

Library of Congress Cataloging-in-Publication Data

Weber, Valerie.
    Traveling in grandma's day / by Valerie Weber and Patricia Anita Baker ; [illustrations by Stuart Lafford].
        p.   cm. - (In grandma's day)
    Includes index.
    Summary: Recalls what it was like to travel from Alaska to Texas as part of a military family in the 1940s and some of the differences in how people got around then and now.
    ISBN 1-57505-326-8 (alk. paper)
    1. United States—Description and travel—Juvenile literature. 2. Travel—Juvenile literature. 3. Baker, Patricia Anita, 1941-   —Journeys—Juvenile literature. 4. Children of military personnel—United States—Biography—Juvenile literature. [1. Travel—History—20th century. 2. United States—Description and travel. 3. Baker, Patricia Anita, 1941-   —Childhood and youth.] I. Baker, Patricia Anita, 1941-   . II. Lafford, Stuart, ill. III. Title. IV. Series: Weber, Valerie. In grandma's day.
E169.W42   1999
917.304'9-dc21   98-12287

Printed in Hong Kong
Bound in the United States of America
1 2 3 4 5 6 - OS - 04 03 02 01 00 99

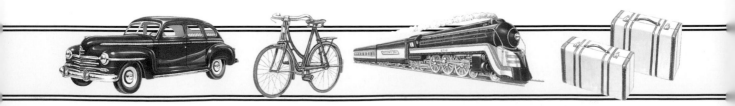

Contents

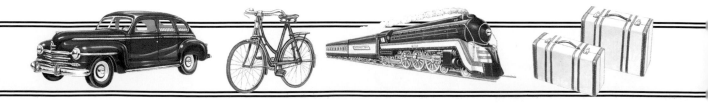

Childhood Travel Time

Hello! My name is Patricia Anita Baker. I live on a small farm near Batavia, Wisconsin. I have one granddaughter named Milissa, who is nine years old, and one grandson, Andrew, who is sixteen. Here I am with both of them and one of my ponies, Blazer.

I was born in Seward, Alaska, in 1941. You can see my house in the photograph on the right. This house was my first home, but I grew up all over the United States. For a while, I even lived in Turkey, a country that lies partly in Europe and partly in Asia.

My dad was in the United States Army. Because the army kept moving him to different jobs in different places, my mother, my two brothers, my sister, and I had to travel a lot to be with him. This family photo was taken when I was seven.

Travel was very different in the 1940s. Would you like to hear more about it?

I was three years old when I took my first long trip. At that time, the United States was fighting against Japan and other countries in World War II. Whenever the U.S. Army thought there was a chance that Japan might invade Alaska, they made our family and other army families evacuate, or leave where we were living. They thought we would be safer out of Alaska.

People who weren't in the army didn't have to leave. By the time I was ten, we had been evacuated three times.

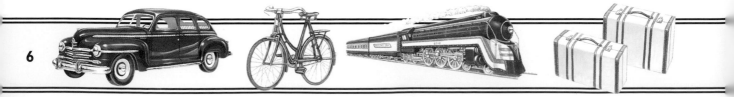

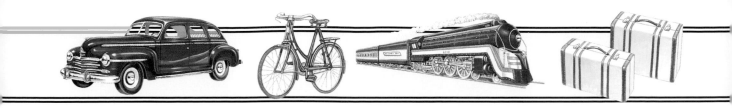

We traveled from Fairbanks, Alaska, in the far northern part of the United States, all the way to Texas, in the southern part of the country. The photo on the right shows me on that journey.

Except for people in the military, few people flew to other countries or distant places in those days. The few people who did travel across the sea went by steamship. We took a steamship like the one in the photo above down the coast of Alaska and Canada to Washington State.

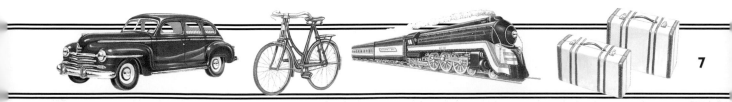

Sailing to Seattle

My whole family stayed in a stateroom, a small room on board the ship with beds attached to the wall. I loved watching the sea through the porthole, the small, round window in our room. In the morning, it was wonderful to go up on deck outside our room to feel the warm sunshine and sea breezes on our faces.

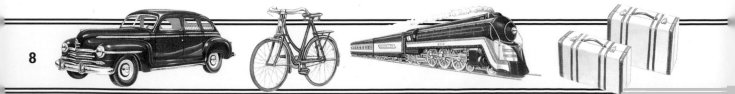

The steamship traveled very close to the Alaskan coastline. It was scary because we were always on the lookout for Japanese submarines that might attack the boat. We had to be very careful about using lights on board the ship at night. No one could smoke a cigarette outside in case an enemy ship noticed the light of the matches.

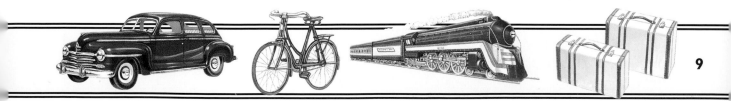

All Aboard!

After we landed in Seattle, Washington, we drove a car to Corvallis, Oregon, where my mother's parents lived. Then my dad and I went by train from Oregon all the way to Columbus, Texas, to see his family. They had never met me before, so it was an exciting visit for all of us!

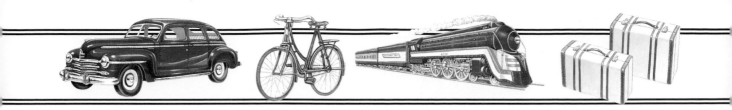

Many things about the train were similar to modern trains, but some things were different. In the 1940s, trains were the main way people traveled long distances. Later, people began to take airplanes instead.

Like modern ones, trains then traveled at about eighty miles per hour between cities, slowing down when they got to areas with lots of people. But they were powered differently back then. In the 1940s, big steam engines fueled by coal or oil both pulled the train and heated and cooled the passenger cars. Modern trains run on diesel fuel, a kind of gasoline, and generators provide the electricity for heating and cooling.

Enjoying the Journey

We bought our tickets at the ticket window in the station, but you could also buy handwritten tickets from a conductor on the train, especially if you didn't need a sleeping berth. You can still buy tickets in a train station, but many people buy them from a travel agent instead.

On our trip, we gave our tickets to a conductor who walked up and down the aisles of the train. I was so excited I could hardly sit still!

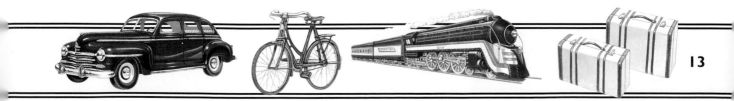

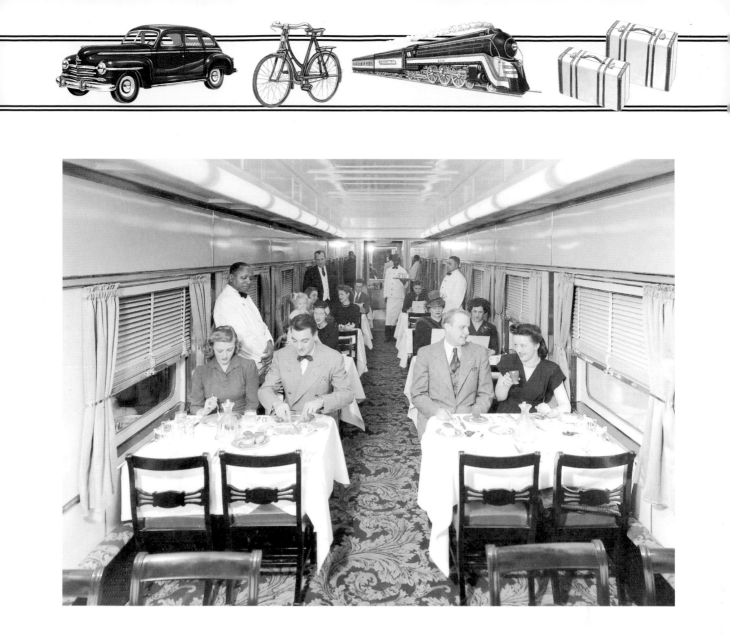

During the day, we sat in double seats that went down both sides of the center aisle of the train. We ate our meals in a separate dining car. A waiter dressed in a sparkling white uniform took our order. In the 1940s, food on the train was cooked on a wood-burning stove.

Long-Distance Travel

Trains had sleeping cars for people who were traveling long distances, as they still do. On modern trains, people who want to sleep in a bed can reserve a private compartment with seats that are turned into beds at night. On my trip to Texas, we slept in a public car that had two sets of beds hanging off the wall, an upper bunk and a lower bunk. I could lie back and look out the window at the town lights flashing by.

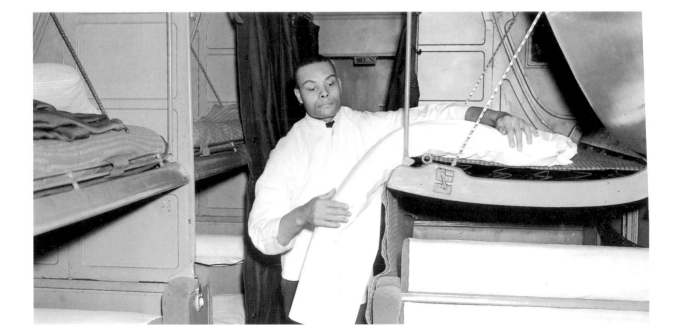

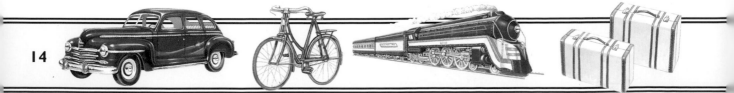

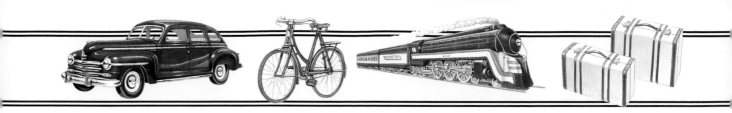

Sometimes we had to wait in train stations for our next train. In the bigger towns, the train stations were huge, with marble floors, wooden ticket windows, and long, hard wooden benches. Many of those stations are still used.

Our trip was 2,700 miles long and took about three days! Once we got to Columbus, Texas, I met my cousins and the rest of my father's relatives. You can see my cousins and me in the photo on the left. I'm the one on the far right.

Getting Around in Alaska

When I was in kindergarten, we moved back to Alaska, to the city of Fairbanks. (That's me standing in the back row in my class photo.) While many big cities in the United States had public transportation such as streetcars and subways, people in the newer cities of the western United States and Alaska drove, biked, or walked to where they were going.

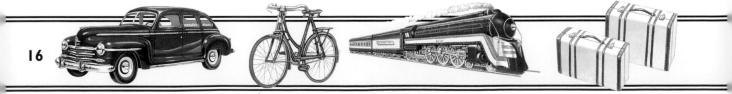

Almost every family in Fairbanks had a car, but gas was rationed during the war so that the military had more gas available for fighting the war. Rationing meant most families got a number of coupons each month for gasoline. No coupons, no gas. My dad was in the military, so we could get as much gas as we needed.

I remember walking to school, sometimes in weather of -40 degrees Fahrenheit. That's more than 70 degrees below freezing! It was really only seven or eight blocks, but the walk felt like it was five miles long.

Sleds and Snowshoes

On special occasions, I got to ride in a dogsled with the local Inuit (also called Eskimos or Native Alaskans). The sled dogs were working dogs, not pets, so you had to be very careful not to get near them or they would nip you.

Many of the Inuit seemed fascinated with my red hair. They said my hair was "as red as the northern lights." (The northern lights are colorful streamers of lights sometimes seen in the northern skies at night.)

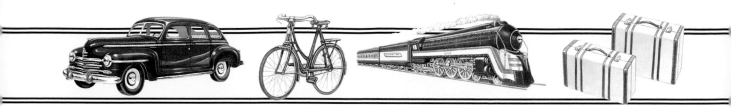

For fun, my father and his friends liked to hike around the wilderness areas of Alaska in snowshoes. You can see my father in his snowshoes in the photo on the left.

Snowshoes look like tennis rackets that you strap to your shoes! They keep you from sinking into deep snow.

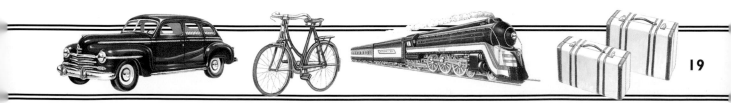

Exploring New Places

When I was in first grade, we moved to Adak Island, the largest in the chain of Aleutian Islands off the coast of Alaska. A big yellow school bus took me to school over dirt roads. It looked almost exactly like the school buses you use. A folding door opened onto steps leading to the bus driver. The low seats were hard and lumpy, and there was a metal bar across the back of the seats.

For my seventh birthday, I got a new bike. It was simple compared to most modern bikes, but I loved it. You can see it below.

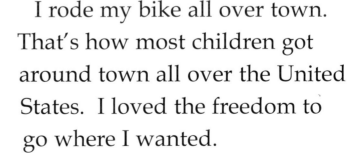

I rode my bike all over town. That's how most children got around town all over the United States. I loved the freedom to go where I wanted.

We also went on lots of car trips when we lived in Alaska. We drove on the Alcan Highway, which went from Fairbanks to the continental United States. You can see the highway in the photo of my mom and me above. Compared to modern paved superhighways, with two, three, or four lanes in each direction, the Alcan was a pretty poor gravel road. And there were no restaurants to eat in or rest stops to use along the way. We had to go to the bathroom in the bushes along the side of the highway.

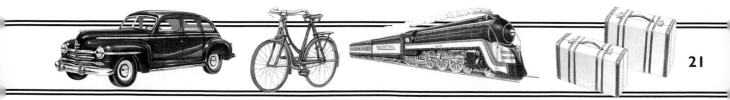

Cars on the Road

When the war ended in 1945, most people were driving cars built before the war. (During the war, most car factories started making war vehicles, like tanks and jeeps, instead of cars.) Many cars did not have heaters or windshield wipers. People wrapped themselves in blankets to stay warm in winter. They also had to stop the car to wipe snow off the windshield. We felt lucky that our gray Plymouth had a heater and windshield wipers.

Our car had a metal dashboard. It had several dials, each with its own arrow showing how fast we were traveling, how much gas we had, and what the engine temperature was. Modern dashboards sometimes also have radios, compact disc players, and clocks. All we had was a cigarette lighter and a radio.

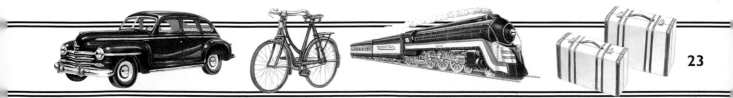

A Great Adventure

My greatest travel adventure of all came when I was eleven. The army told my family to move to Ankara, Turkey. We traveled by car, bus, airplane, ferry, and train.

We started our journey with my uncle, who drove us from Seattle, Washington, to New York. The roads across the United States were mostly two-lane highways with houses and farms at the road's edge. Unlike modern freeways that go around towns, these roads went right through the middle of every town along the way. It was interesting to see the different towns speed past our windows.

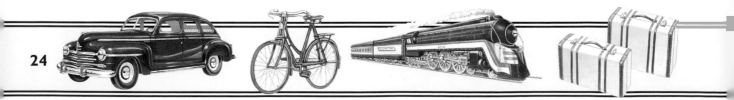

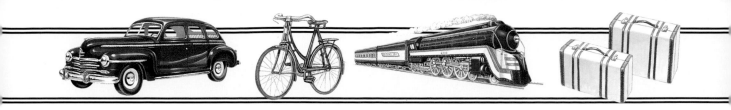

Gas stations were different, too. In the 1940s and 1950s, people didn't pump their own gas: gas station attendants pumped gas for them, cleaned the windshield, and checked the oil. Instead of many gas pumps holding three different kinds of gas, there was usually only one pump and one kind of gas.

Restaurants and motels also stood at the side of the road. Motels were usually cottages that people rented overnight while they traveled. We didn't have the money to spend on motels and restaurants. Instead we timed the length of each day's journey so that we could stop at different relatives' homes each night. Every day we would stop for a picnic lunch.

From New York to Turkey

Once in New York, we had to travel from one air force base to another in a bus to get our passport photo, which you can see here. We used both military and civilian buses, but they all seemed alike. Without air conditioning, they were very noisy and smelly because the exhaust fumes from the motor came in through the open windows.

A few days after arriving in New York, we got on a plane to begin our trip to Turkey. Planes were powered by propellers then instead of by jets. They were so noisy and bumpy that we could not hear each other speak!

When you're flying, the higher you go, the less oxygen there is and the harder it is to breathe. If you've flown in a plane, the air in the passenger cabin was controlled so there was plenty of oxygen. When I was young, the air in the plane could not be controlled, so we couldn't go too high.

1940 and now

TWA FIRST TO BRING YOU:

4 Engines!
Supercharged Cabin!
Overweather Flying!

Boeing

— *The TRANSCONTINENTAL Airline* —

TWA *Stratoliner*

TWA *Stratoliner*

High altitude *Outside*
Low altitude *Inside*

FLY OUT OF REACH OF EARTH-BOUND WEATHER!

TWA
The TRANSCONTINENTAL Airline

-TO-COAST . . . NOW HOURS FASTER!

We could easily see the lights on the coastline as we left. We flew at about 150 miles per hour.

Modern passenger planes fly over 570 miles per hour at 35,000 feet, high above the clouds. It took us three days to travel by plane, train, and ferry from New York to Turkey, a trip that would take only twelve hours by modern airplane.

Travel: The Good Parts and Bad

At times, it was hard to travel so much as a child. I had to leave my friends and learn about new places. And I was always the new kid in school, which was difficult.

But I learned a lot from traveling. I learned that people live in many ways and that I could be friends with people who live and think very differently from me. I feel lucky to have met so many people from other cultures and to have seen places where few Americans had been. I still love to travel. But I also enjoy coming home and staying in one place for a while. That is, until I go off on my next adventure, of course!

Glossary

cabin: a place in the middle of the airplane for passengers, aircrew, and sometimes cargo. The pilot sits in the cockpit, a separate room in the front of the plane.

deck: the floor of a ship or boat

evacuate: to leave someplace, usually because of danger

exhaust: the used gases that escape from the back of an engine

ferry: a boat used to carry people, goods, and vehicles across a narrow body of water

generator: a machine that produces electricity or other forms of energy

lookout: a careful watch for something or somebody

passport: a booklet showing that you are a citizen of a particular country. It also gives you permission to travel to other countries.

rationing: limiting to fixed portions. When certain items are scarce, sometimes the government limits how many of those items people can buy.

streetcar: a vehicle for carrying people, powered by electric wires strung along a street

subway: a railroad under the streets and buildings of a city

For Further Reading

Bellville, Cheryl Walsh. *The Airplane Book*. Minneapolis, Minn.: Carolrhoda Books, Inc., 1991.

Duden, Jane. *Timeline:* 1940s. New York: Crestwood House, 1989.

Otfinoksi, Steve. *Behind the Wheel: Cars Then and Now.* New York: Benchmark Books, 1997.

Otfinoksi, Steve. *Riding the Rails: Trains Then and Now.* New York: Benchmark Books, 1997.

Whitman, Sylvia. *Get Up and Go: The History of American Road Travel.* Minneapolis, Minn.: Lerner Publications Co., 1996.

Whitman, Sylvia. *V Is for Victory: The American Home Front During World War II.* Minneapolis, Minn.: Lerner Publications Co., 1993.

Wilkinson, Phillip & Michael Pollardo. *Transportation.* New York: Chelsea House, 1995.

For permission to reproduce copyrighted material, the authors and publishers gratefully acknowledge the following: Advertising Archives: 27, cover (back, bottom); Archive Photos: 8; Archive Photos/Muir: 26 (bottom); Archive Photos/Peter Sickles: 15 (top); Brown Brothers: 24; Corbis Bettman: 6; FPG: 7 (middle), 20 (middle right); H. Armstrong Roberts: 18 (middle right), 25; Milwaukee County Historical Society: 9; Peter Newark's Historical Pictures: 11, 22; Stock Montage, Inc.: 13, 17 (top), 29 (top), cover (front); UPI/Corbis-Bettmann: 10, 12, 14.

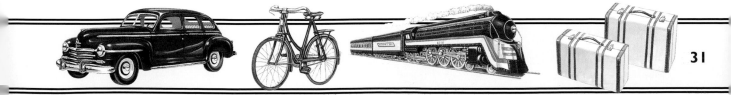

Index

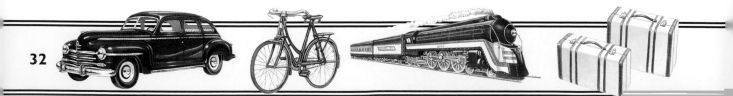